CW01401486

CAN YOU MAKE A

PILLOW

OUT OF

GLASS?

by Susan B. Katz

raintree
a Capstone company — publishers for children

Raintree is an imprint of Capstone Global Library Limited, a company incorporated in
England and Wales having its registered office at 264 Banbury Road, Oxford, OX2 7DY –
Registered company number: 6695582

www.raintree.co.uk
myorders@raintree.co.uk

Edited by Christianne Jones
Designed by Elyse White
Original illustrations © Capstone Global Library Limited 2023
Picture research by Morgan Walters
Production by Polly Fisher
Originated by Capstone Global Library Ltd

978 1 3982 4786 4 (hardback)
978 1 3982 4785 7 (paperback)

British Library Cataloguing in Publication Data
A full catalogue record for this book is available from the British Library.

Acknowledgements
We would like to thank the following for permission to reproduce photographs: Shutterstock:
Africa Studio, 15, biDaala studio, 16, CREATISTA, 9, Epov Dmitry, 21, fizkes, 17, Freeograph,
5, Hung Chung Chih, 19, Ivelin Denev, 10, Monkey Business Images, 13, New Africa, (left)
Cover, noprati somchit, 7, Skylines, 11, uchka, (right) Cover, yosmoes815, 8

Every effort has been made to contact copyright holders of material reproduced in this book.
Any omissions will be rectified in subsequent printings if notice is given to the publisher.

All the internet addresses (URLs) given in this book were valid at the time of going to press.
However, due to the dynamic nature of the internet, some addresses may have changed, or
sites may have changed or ceased to exist since publication. While the author and publisher
regret any inconvenience this may cause readers, no responsibility for any such changes can
be accepted by either the author or the publisher.

Contents

Words in **bold** are in the glossary.

A glass pillow?

Pillows are meant to support your head and neck while you sleep. They can be **firm** or soft. Pillows can have different materials inside them, such as feathers, cotton or **polyester**.

So would glass make a good material for a pillow? Let's find out more!

Properties of glass

Glass is a hard, clear material. It can be thick or thin. It does not bend easily. But it can break easily.

Glass is strong and can be made almost everywhere in the world. It can be made into large sheets. Little pieces of glass can be shaped into other things.

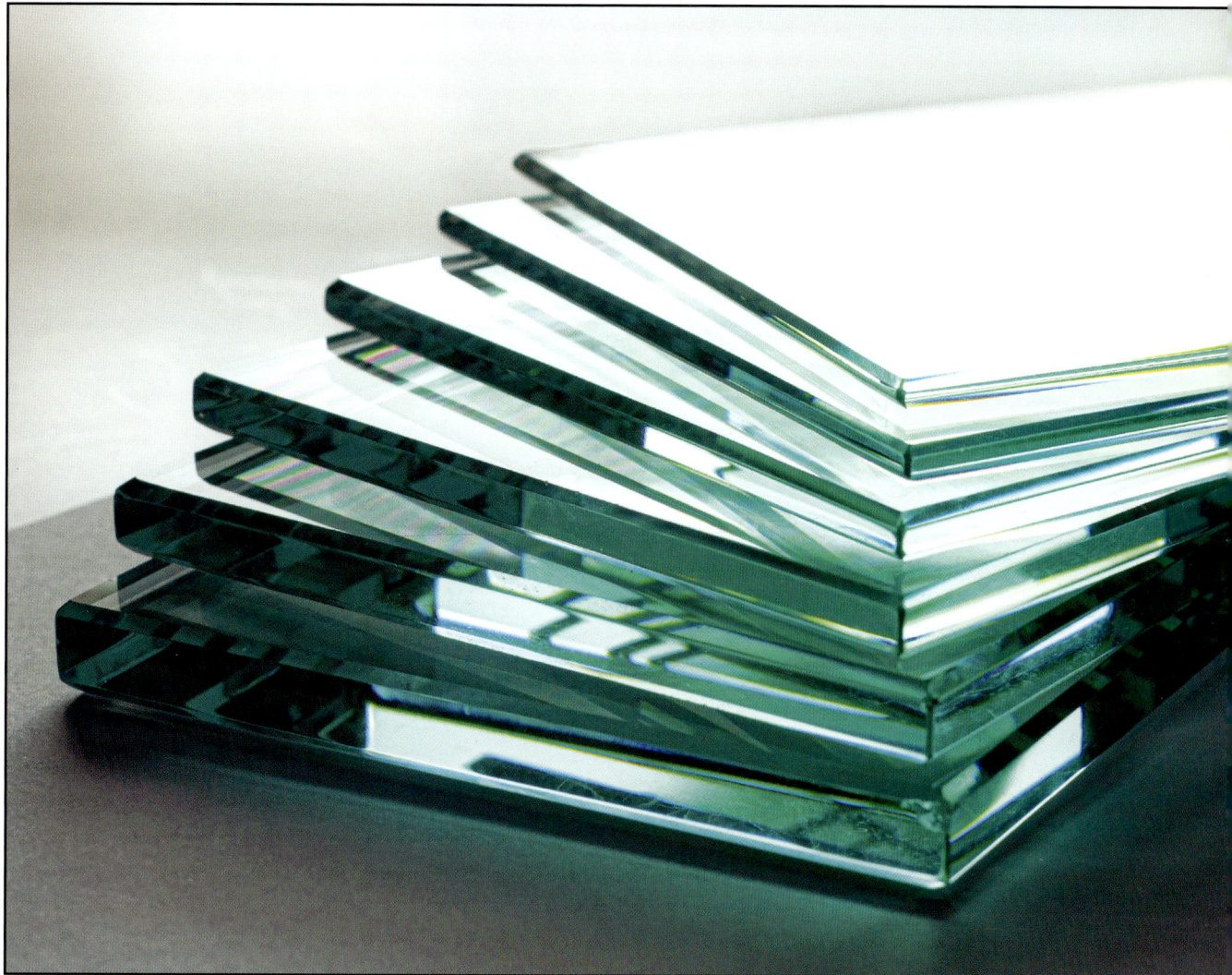

Six different sizes of glass sheets stacked up.

Glass is made from natural materials such as sand and limestone. When melted, these materials reach a very high temperature. Then, they combine to form a new material. That material is glass.

Materials being melted to make glass.

Glass being made into a vase.

When it is hot, glass acts like a liquid.
But at room temperature it becomes a solid.

Most glass is see-through or clear. Some glass can be **tinted** to be a darker colour. You might see tinted windows on office buildings or cars.

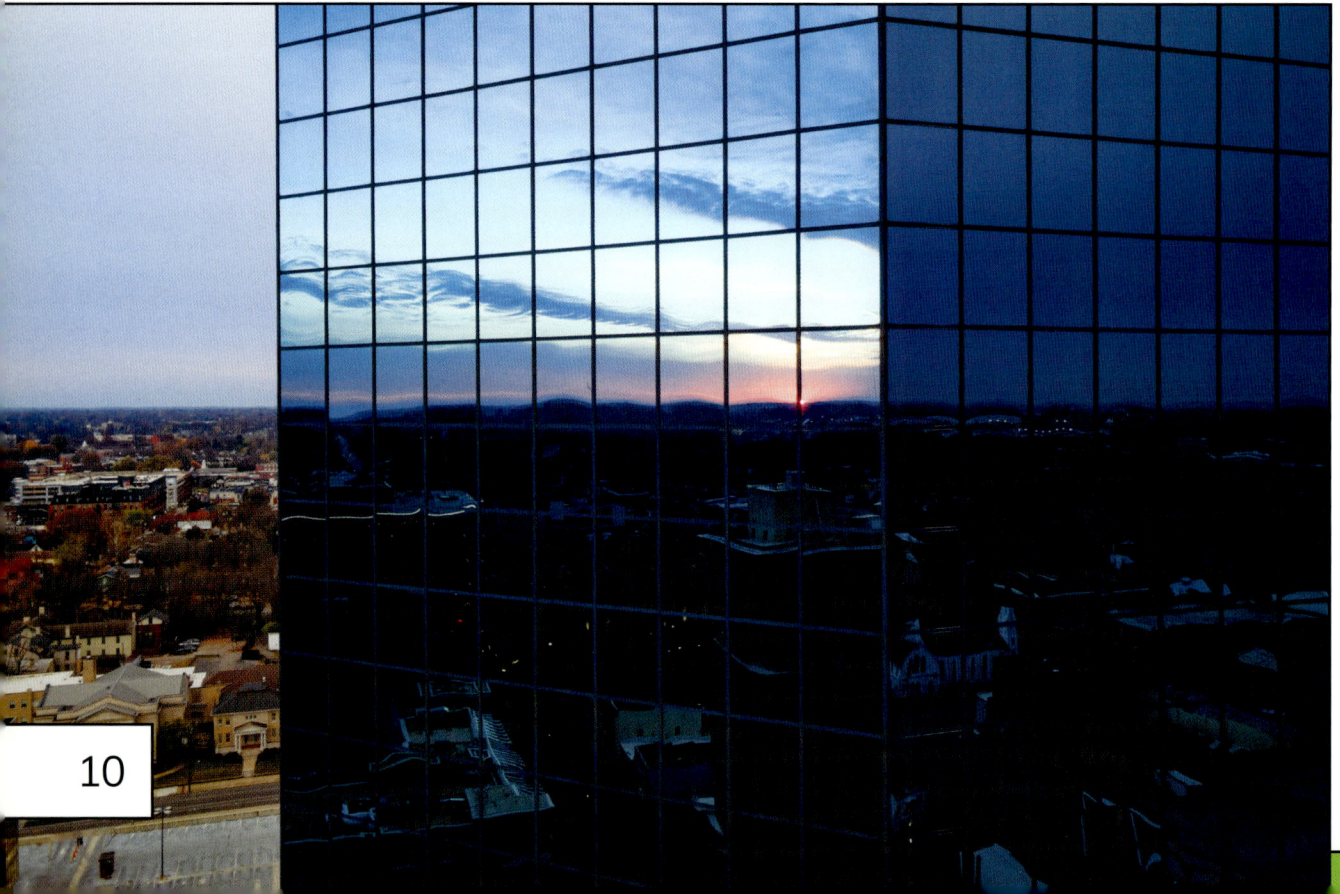

Glass can also be reused or **recycled**. It is important to recycle and help the Earth.

Made from glass

Glass can be big. The most common use for large glass is windows and mirrors. It is used in car windscreens and office buildings too.

Glass protects people from the cold, rain and wind. It lets light in at the same time.

Glass can be small. Drinking glasses and bottles are some of the most common uses for glass. Glass bottles can be **insulated** to keep the liquid inside cold or hot.

Lots of food is put into glass jars. We make jars out of glass because it is solid, but we can still see through it. It can be sealed to keep food fresh.

Computers, phones and tablets all have glass screens. Scientists use glass **beakers** in labs. Light bulbs are glass, and so are car headlights. Cameras use glass, and X-ray machines do too.

Glass and pillows

Glass is found in items all around you, but it is hard and can shatter. It doesn't bend easily, so it wouldn't be very comfortable.

When you lay down at night, think about putting your head on a hard, cold glass surface. Would you have sweet dreams?

So could you make a pillow out of glass? Would you?

ACTIVITY

Growing in glass

A glass container is perfect for growing plants. It is see-through so you can watch the plant grow. It will also let light in. It is solid so it will hold water too.

What you need:

- a bottle, jar or other small glass container

- soil (enough to fill up your container)

- plant or flower seeds

What to do:

1. Fill up your container with soil.

2. Dig a small hole and plant your seeds or plants.

3. Cover the hole back up with soil.

4. Place your jar near a window.

5. Water your plant according to directions for the seed/plant and watch it grow in glass.

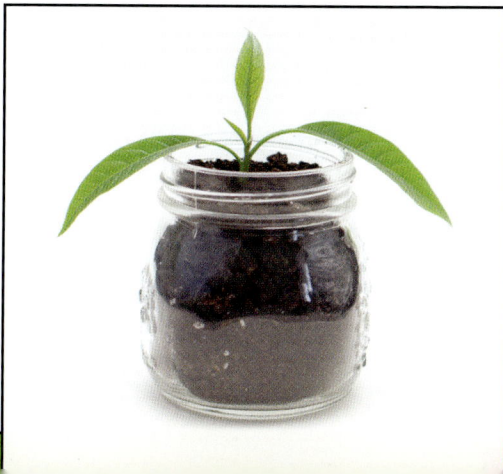

Glossary

beaker glass cup or tube used to hold liquids

firm hard

insulate cover a material so it stays hot or cold

polyester man-made material used to make clothing, sheets and pillows

recycle make used items into new products

tint make a lighter or darker shade of a colour

Find out more

Books

Amazing Materials: Solids, Liquids and Gases, Rob Colson (Wayland, 2019)

Everyday Materials (Ways Into Science), Peter Riley (Franklin Watts, 2016)

Experiments with Materials (Read and Experiment), Isabel Thomas (Raintree, 2016)

Websites

www.bbc.co.uk/bitesize/topics/z6p6qp3/ articles/zx8hhv4

Learn more about materials and their properties.

www.dkfindout.com/uk/science/materials

Find out more about all sorts of materials and take a materials quiz!

Index

About the author

Susan B. Katz is an award-winning Spanish bilingual author, National Board Certified Teacher, educational consultant and social media strategist. When she's not writing, Susan enjoys salsa dancing and spending time at the beach.